TIM FLACH

Who Am I?

A Peek-Through-Pages Book
of Endangered Animals

Abrams Books for Young Readers • New York

in association with

Blackwell&Ruth.

I have a black furry mask, and I'm naturally shy.
I spend nearly fourteen hours a day eating and
can weigh up to three hundred pounds!

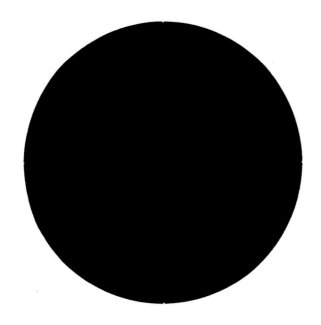

Who am I?

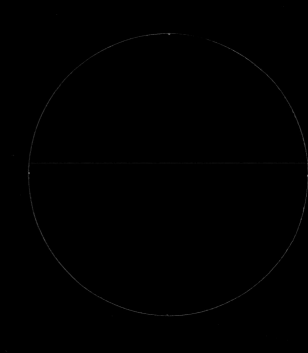

I am a giant panda

I have the best of both worlds—
on the land and in the water.
Some people say I'm a walking fish.

Who am I?

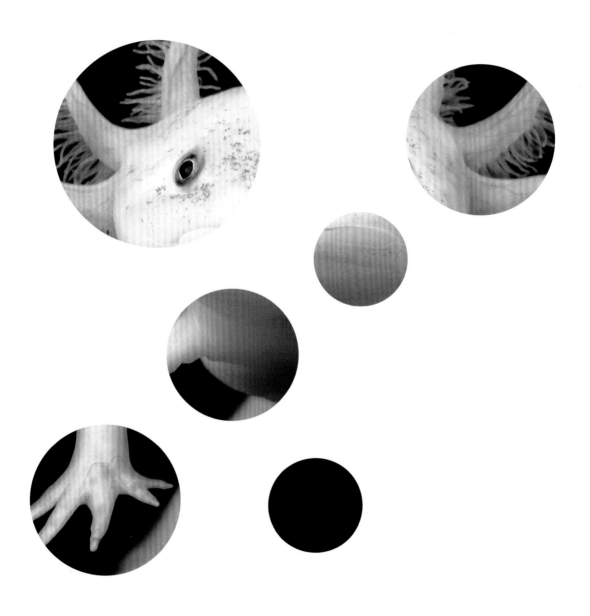

I am an axolotl.

I'm the only sea bear in the world.
You might think my home is freezing,
but without the ice, I can't survive.

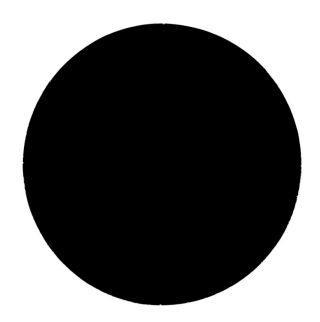

Who am I?

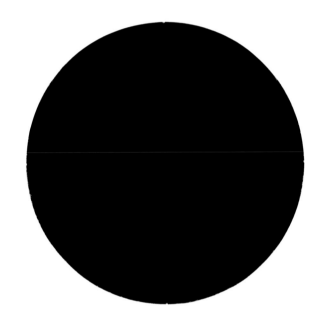

I am a polar bear.

I am a gentle giant with a heart-shaped nose. You might think that I eat only bananas, but I dine on all kinds of fruit and even the occasional termite in my African rain forest home.

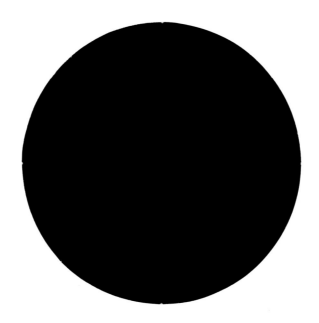

Who am I?

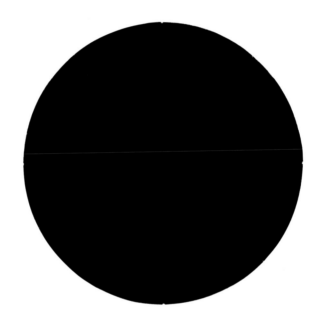

I am a western
lowland gorilla.

It can be hard to spot me between the leaves, but if you look carefully you might see my big yellow eyes. I have very long legs and suction pads on my toes that make me an excellent jumper.

Who am I?

I am a yellow-eyed tree frog.

I build my nest at the top of the highest tree. When I need to feed my family, I swoop down and snatch up a passing snack. Care to share a flying squirrel sandwich?

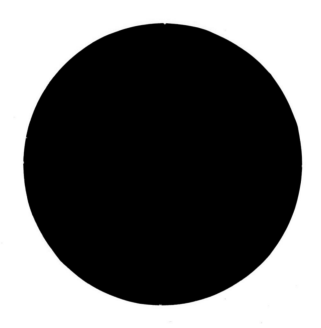

Who am I?

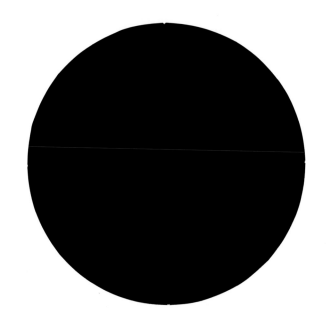

I am a Philippine eagle.

I may be a very big cat,
but you won't hear me meow.
My roar can be heard from miles away.

Who am I?

I am a Bengal tiger.

I have a suit of armor
and a super-long tongue
for slurping up insects—yum!

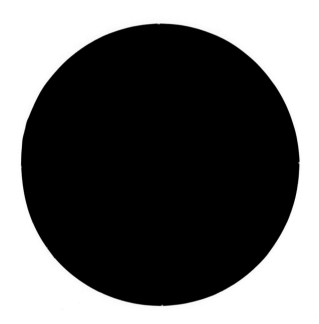

Who am I?

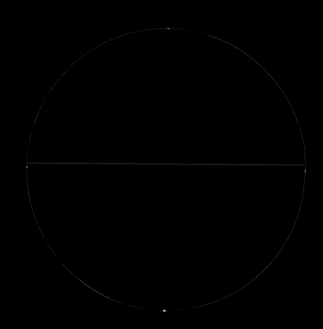

I am a white-bellied pangolin.

I'm a priceless, living work of art with my patterned black-and-gold shell. I'm known for being a bit slow, so when a predator comes my way I tuck my head and limbs inside my shell to stay safe.

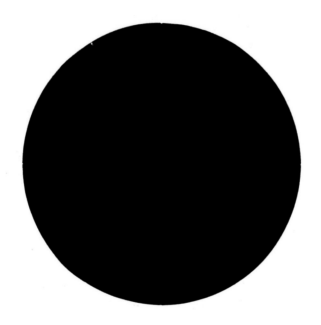

Who am I?

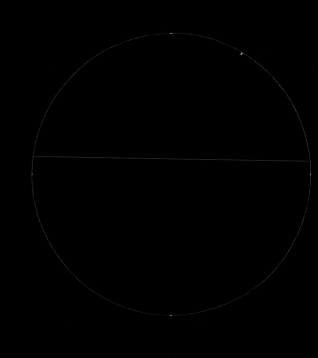

I am a ploughshare
tortoise.

I'm a gorgeous glider with a multicolored fur coat and a very long tail. Watch me leap from tree to tree.

Who am I?

I am a crowned sifaka.

Who are we?

I am a sea angel.

I am a giant panda.

What makes me so special?

You might think I have wings, but those are my fins. They help me move through the water. You'll find me all over the place—in cold polar seas and also in tropical waters. And what do sea angels eat? Sea butterflies, of course—I fire tentacles out of my face to catch them.

What makes me so special?

I am a bear, but I mainly eat bamboo—lots and lots of it. That's why they call me the bamboo bear. I live in cool, wet bamboo forests in the mountains of China.

Why are we endangered?

There's less food for us to eat, because the sea is too acidic. Sea butterflies are actually a type of snail, and pollution is causing their shells to dissolve. If sea butterflies die out, we won't have anything to eat.

Why are we endangered?

While we aren't endangered anymore, we're still under serious threat. Our forests have been cleared to make roads and railroads for people. If there are no bamboo forests, we can't survive. There's some good news, though! Our government has made lots of nature reserves to protect us, and our numbers are slowly increasing.

I am an axolotl.

I am a polar bear.

What makes me so special?
Those aren't feathers on my head; they're gills to help me breathe underwater. I have amazing healing powers. If I lose a leg, I'll just grow a new one.

Why are we endangered?
Humans introduced big fish, such as carp, to our lakes and canals in Mexico City. The fish ate all our food! Then our water was polluted by humans, and we couldn't survive in the wild anymore. The only places you'll find us now are at an aquarium, science lab, or pet shop.

What makes me so special?
My giant paws help me to swim long distances and stand on the thin ice in my Arctic home. My coat looks white, but it's actually made out of clear hollow tubes filled with air. Underneath my coat, my skin is black, which makes it easier for me to absorb the sun's rays and stay warm.

Why are we endangered?
The climate is heating up, causing the sea ice to melt. This makes it harder for us to catch seals. If we can't eat, we go hungry.

I am a western lowland gorilla.

What makes me so special?

You'll find me living with a whole troop of gorillas. We can climb trees, but mostly you'll find us on the ground, building nests out of branches, eating, and hanging out. Young gorillas like to play games such as tag. You're it!

Why are we endangered?

People hunt us for our meat and chop down our forests to make room for farmland and more houses. Then we have nowhere to live. There's also a virus called Ebola that is making us sick. Scientists are working hard to create a vaccine to protect us from it.

I am a yellow-eyed tree frog.

What makes me so special?

I lay my eggs in the trees above a pond. When the eggs hatch, tiny tadpoles drop into the water. They grow arms and legs and turn into frogs. Then they hop into the trees.

Why are we endangered?

Our leafy homes in Costa Rica have been cut down to make more homes for people. How can you be a tree frog if you don't have a tree? Come on, guys, let's share!

I am a
Philippine eagle.

What makes me so special?
I am one of the biggest eagles in the whole world, with a wingspan of up to seven feet! See how the feathers on my head are sticking up? It means I'm paying attention to YOU!

Why are we endangered?
Our forests were chopped down so humans could sell logs and make more room for farms and towns. Forest fires have also destroyed our homes. In the Philippines, people are working hard to save us. We've even been made our country's national bird!

I am a
Bengal tiger.

What makes me so special?
I'm one of a kind—no other tiger has stripes like mine. I'm an excellent hunter. I sneak up silently on my prey and then . . . POUNCE!

Why are we endangered?
People hunt us for our stripy coats, to make medicine, and because they think we bring them luck. *We* think it's lucky to be alive! Most of us live in India, but you'll also find us in other parts of Southeast Asia. We roam great distances to hunt our food, but our habitat has become a lot smaller because humans have cleared it to build more towns and cities.

I am a
white-bellied pangolin.

What makes me so special?

You'll find me in Asia and Africa. I am the only mammal in the world with scales to protect me from predators like big cats. When I'm scared, I roll up into a ball. There are two photos of me in this book. Can you find the picture of me clinging to my mother's tail?

Why are we endangered?

People eat us and make medicines from us. They even make handbags out of us! You can help save us by celebrating World Pangolin Day on the third Saturday of every February.

I am a
ploughshare tortoise.

What makes me so special?

I'm one of the rarest reptiles in the world. You'll find me only near Baie de Baly in Madagascar. I eat all kinds of plants, but grasses are my favorite. When it's time to find a mate, the males fight over the females. The aim is to flip your opponent over onto his shell. *En garde!*

Why are we endangered?

Conservationists are working hard to save our species. They even engrave numbers into our shells so poachers don't steal us. Our shells are very hard, so this doesn't hurt us at all. Instead it keeps us safe.

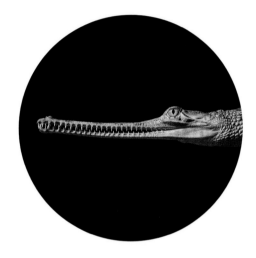

I am a
crowned sifaka.

I am an
Indian gharial.

What makes me so special?

I get around by leaping from tree to tree.
With my powerful hind legs I can jump more
than thirty feet! I don't come down to the
ground very often, but when I do, I hop along
with my arms outstretched for balance.

What makes me so special?

My long, skinny snout helps me to sense
vibrations in the water. I wait until I can
feel a fish swimming beside me, then
I whip my head from side to side and
snap it up with one bite.

Why are we endangered?

People cut down our forest homes in
Madagascar and hunt us for our meat
and fur, but we deserve to be treated like
royalty—check out my furry black crown.
Sometimes people take us away to be pets,
but we belong with our families in the forest.

Why are we endangered?

People have changed the way our rivers
flow so that they can use our water, too,
but sometimes there's not enough water
left for us to live in. We also get tangled
up in fishing nets and can't escape.

Wanted! Caretakers for Planet Earth—
How You Can Help

All the animals in this book are endangered or threatened, which means that if we don't try to save them, there won't be any more of them on our planet. Imagine if there were no more Bengal tigers, monarch butterflies, or ring-tailed lemurs! Lots of people are working hard to try to save endangered and threatened species, and you can help, too, even if you live on the other side of the world from some of these creatures. Here are some ideas about what you can do at home:

Use Less Energy

Humans are using so much electricity, water, and gas that it is causing our planet to warm up too much. This is called global warming, and it has changed many animals' habitats, greatly reducing their chances of survival. Global warming has caused the ice that polar bears live on to melt earlier every year, making it harder for them to catch food. You can help slow down global warming by turning the tap off when you brush your teeth, riding a bike or walking instead of traveling by car, turning lights off when you're not using them, and not leaving the refrigerator door open for longer than you need to. Can you think of other ways to use less energy?

Reduce, Reuse, Recycle

When forests are cut down to make more room for farms and cities, the creatures who live in them have nowhere to go and nothing to eat. Many governments are making laws to stop forests from being cut down so that animals have somewhere to live. One way you can help is by using products made from recycled paper. This means that fewer trees will have to be cut down to make new paper. In addition to paper to write and draw on, you can buy tissues, toilet paper, and napkins made from recycled paper.

Our oceans are filled with plastic, and it's harming our sea creatures. Use cloth shopping bags instead of plastic, choose items at the supermarket with less plastic packaging, and don't use plastic straws.

Support Conservation Projects

Visit wildlife centers and sanctuaries that are working hard to protect endangered species.

When you visit these places, money from the tickets they sell goes toward the creatures they are trying to protect. You also learn more about our endangered creatures and can help spread the word!

Some animals, particularly some types of parrots such as macaws, have become endangered because people have removed them from their habitats to make them pets. But they belong in the rain forest! Instead of buying an exotic pet from a pet store, why not adopt an endangered animal or two online? They won't live at your house, but you'll be able to look at photos of them and get updates about how they're doing. Websites such as wwf.panda.org can help you with online adoptions.

Support Neighborhood Wildlife

No matter where you live, remember that nature is all around us. Encourage wildlife by planting native plants, flowers, and trees in your backyard or community garden. This provides food for bees and butterflies and creates homes for toads and frogs. Avoid all pesticides and herbicides! You can also help wildlife by picking up trash around your neighborhood or when you're at the beach.

Check out endangered.org/10-easy-things-you-can-do-to-save-endangered-species for more ideas.

Be a Voice

Don't be afraid to speak out and spread the word about protecting endangered species. For real change to occur, global action is needed. Encourage the people in your life to think about how they can help create positive change. Visit wwf.panda.org to see what you can do.

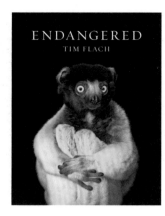

Tim Flach

Tim Flach is a photographer best known for his portraits of animals and for the originality that he brings to capturing animal behavior. In recognition of his work, he has received numerous awards, and his photographs are showcased in books, exhibitions, and galleries around the world. Tim has photographed some of the most threatened species on Earth to create the images for his Endangered series. At a panda research center in China, he photographed giant panda Ya Yun, who tore Tim's crushed velvet backdrop into two pieces before settling down for her photo shoot. After spending days searching for a Philippine eagle in the mountains of the Philippine islands, he gave up trying to find one in the wild and photographed one at a wildlife sanctuary there instead. Back at home in London, he has two Burmese cats named Blue and Hunt, who like to watch him work, and three goldfish. He believes that community-based conservation and enhancing feelings of kinship between humans and animals are important factors in saving some of our most threatened species.

timflach.com | @timflachphotography

Library of Congress Control Number 2018960406
ISBN 978-1-4197-3646-9

Produced and originated by
Blackwell and Ruth Limited
Suite 405 IronBank, 150 Karangahape Road,
Auckland 1010, New Zealand
blackwellandruth.com

Images originally published in *Endangered* by Tim Flach, copyright © 2017 Tim Flach
Text, design, and concept copyright
© 2019 Blackwell & Ruth Ltd.
Text by Rachel Clare

Printed and bound in China
10 9 8 7 6 5 4 3 2 1

Abrams Books for Young Readers are available at special discounts when purchased in quantity for premiums and promotions as well as fundraising or educational use. Special editions can also be created to specification. For details, contact specialsales@abramsbooks.com or the address below.

Abrams® is a registered trademark of Harry N. Abrams, Inc.

This book is made with FSC®-certified paper and other controlled material and is printed with soy vegetable inks. The Forest Stewardship Council® (FSC®) is a global, not-for-profit organization dedicated to the promotion of responsible forest management worldwide to meet the social, ecological, and economic rights and needs of the present generation without compromising those of future generations.

MIX
Paper from
responsible sources
FSC® C016973

ABRAMS The Art of Books
195 Broadway, New York, NY 10007
abramsbooks.com